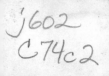

creative crafts from
cardboard tubes

By Nikki Connor

Illustrated by Sarah-Jane Neaves

Copper Beech Books
Brookfield, Connecticut

© Aladdin Books Ltd 1997
Designed and produced by
Aladdin Books Ltd
28 Percy Street
London W1P 0LD

First published in the United States
in 1997 by
Copper Beech Books,
an imprint of
The Millbrook Press
2 Old New Milford Road
Brookfield, Connecticut 06804

Design David West Children's Book
Design
Illustrator Sarah-Jane Neaves
Photographer Roger Vlitos

Printed in Belgium

Library of Congress Cataloging-in-
Publication Data

Connor, Nikki. Cardboard Tubes / by Nikki
Connor ; illustrated by Sarah-Jane Neaves.
     p. cm. -- (Creative crafts from--)
     Summary: Provides
instructions for making such items as a
haunted house, princess puppet, pencil
holder, and marble run from cardboard
tubes of various shapes and sizes.
     ISBN 0-7613-0552-1 (lib. bdg.)
  1. Paper toy making--Juvenile literature.
  2. Paperboard--Recycling--Juvenile
literature. [1. Paper toy making.
          2. Handicraft.]
I. Neaves, Sarah-Jane, ill. II. Title. III. Series:
  Connor, Nikki. Creative crafts from--
TT174.5.P3C66   1997   96-45582
745.54--dc21   CIP AC

Contents

Before you start

A "what you need" ingredients panel appears with the photograph of each project. Decide which project you are going to make and collect everything you need.

 The red, yellow, and blue paint cups mean that you need poster paints. All colors (except white) can be made by mixing together a combination of these three. See the color chart at the back of this book to find out how. You may choose instead to use ready mixed colors if you have them.

 Use a pencil point to punch holes in paper or thin plastic. For thicker cardboard and plastic, you may need to use scissors - <u>ask an adult to help</u>.

A dotted line in the instructions means you are to fold, not cut. A solid line shows where to cut.

Only use scissors that are especially designed for children's crafts. They usually have rounded ends. Always have an adult with you when you use them.

 Where a project needs colored paper remember you may use any color you choose. If you have none, use white paper and paint it!

If you follow the step-by-step instructions carefully you will be sure to finish up with a successful model - but if you prefer to use these designs just as ideas to get you started, then that's fine too!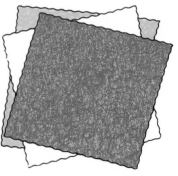

Have fun.

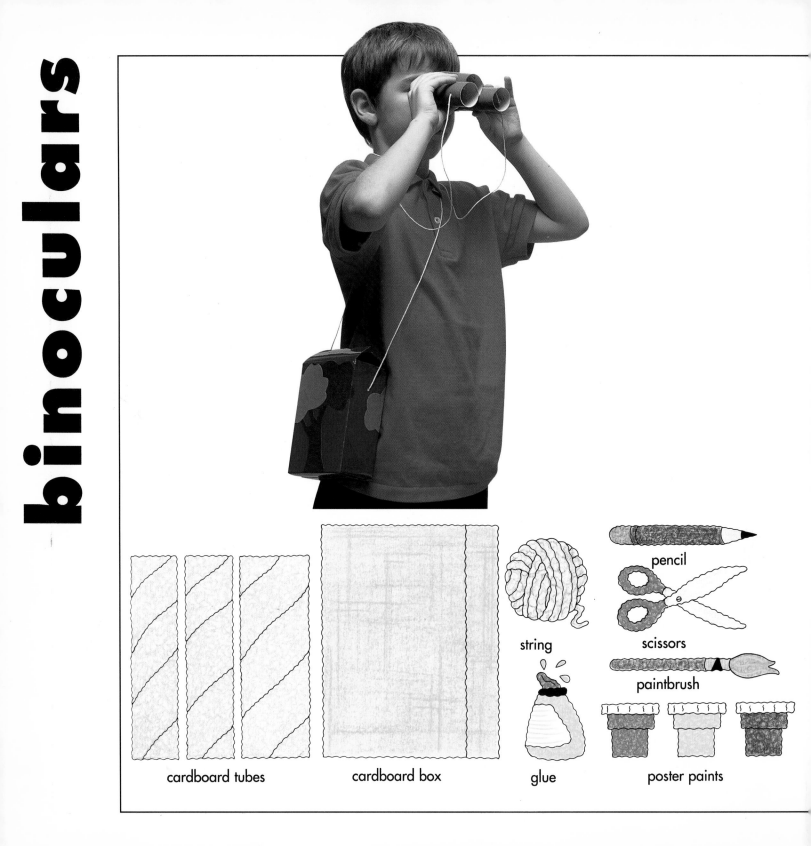

binoculars

cardboard tubes

cardboard box

string

glue

pencil

scissors

paintbrush

poster paints

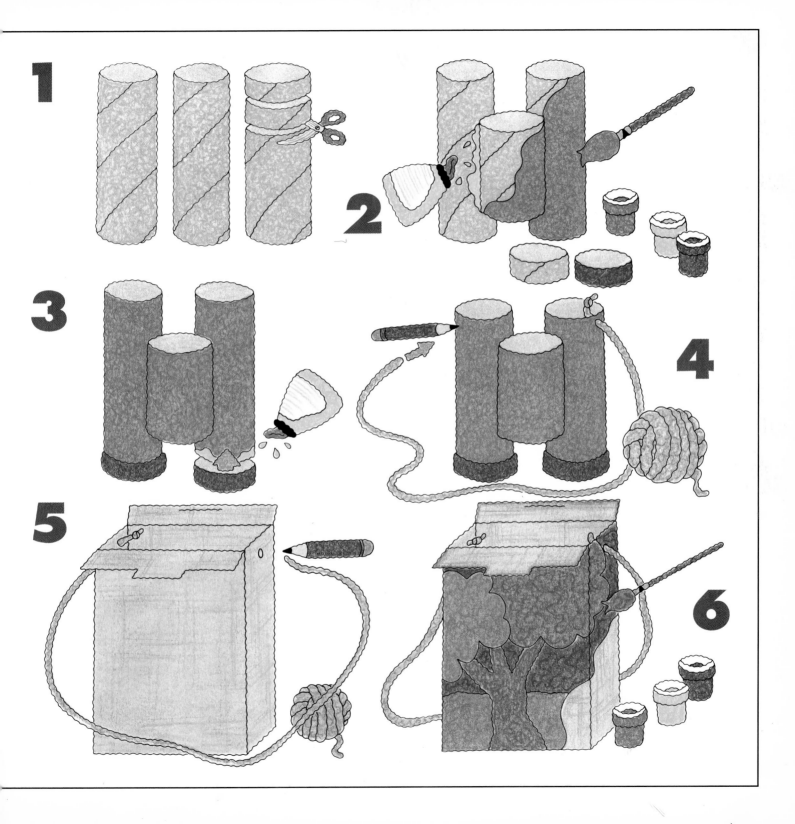

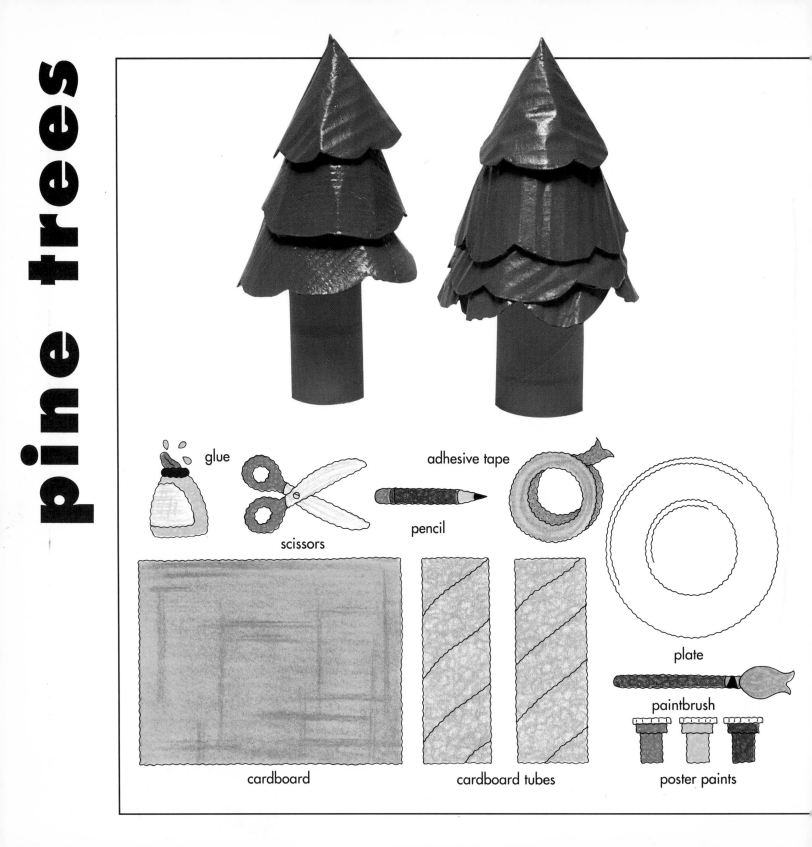

pine trees

glue

scissors

pencil

adhesive tape

plate

cardboard

cardboard tubes

paintbrush

poster paints

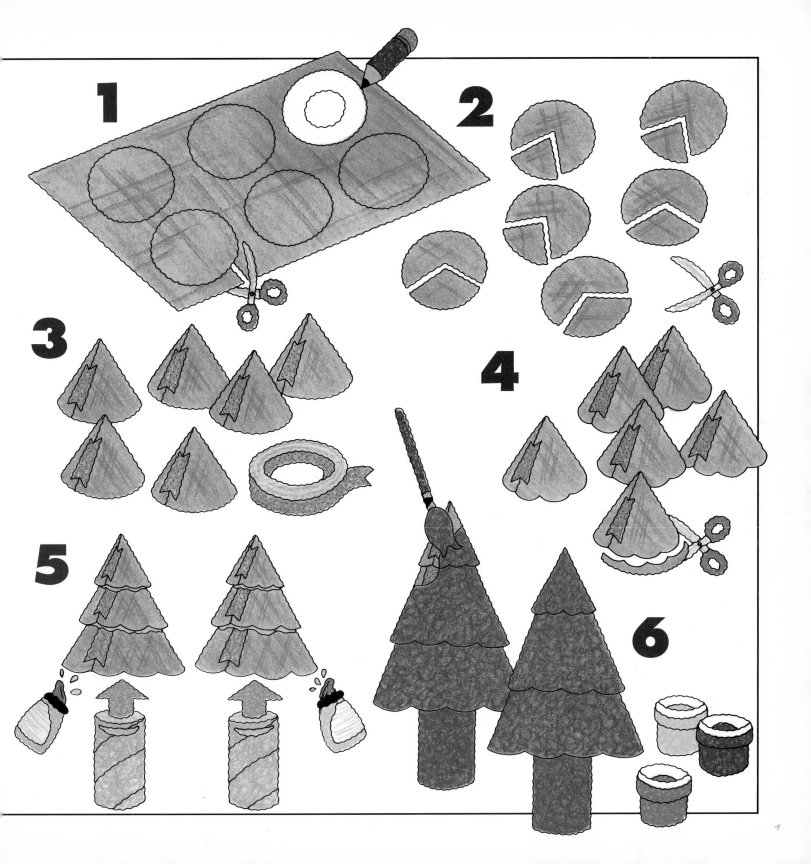

1

2

3

4

5

6

tepee

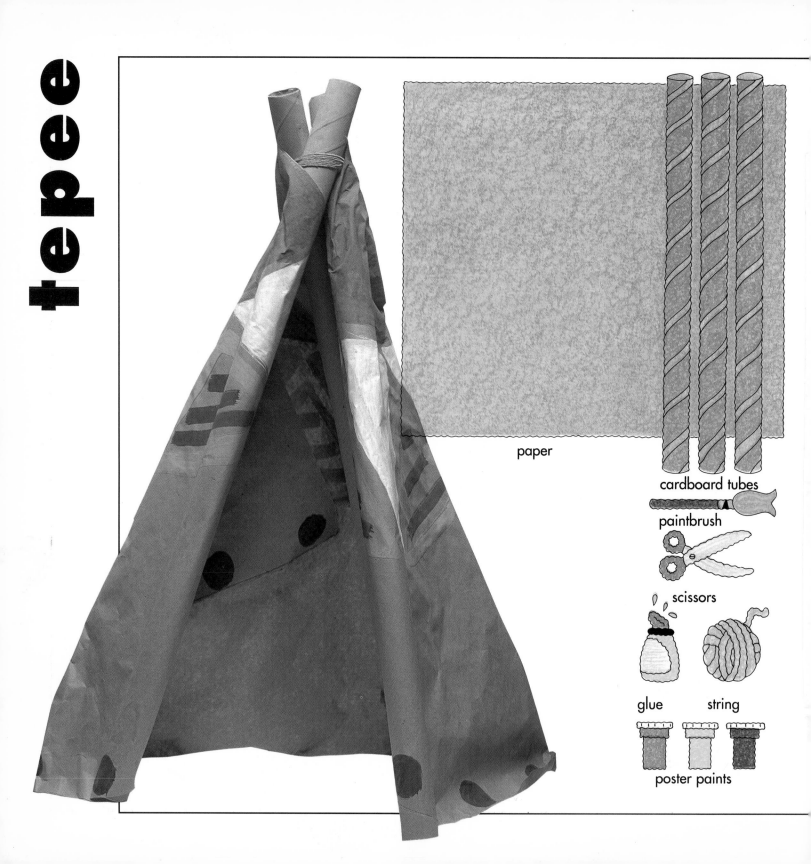

paper

cardboard tubes

paintbrush

scissors

glue   string

poster paints

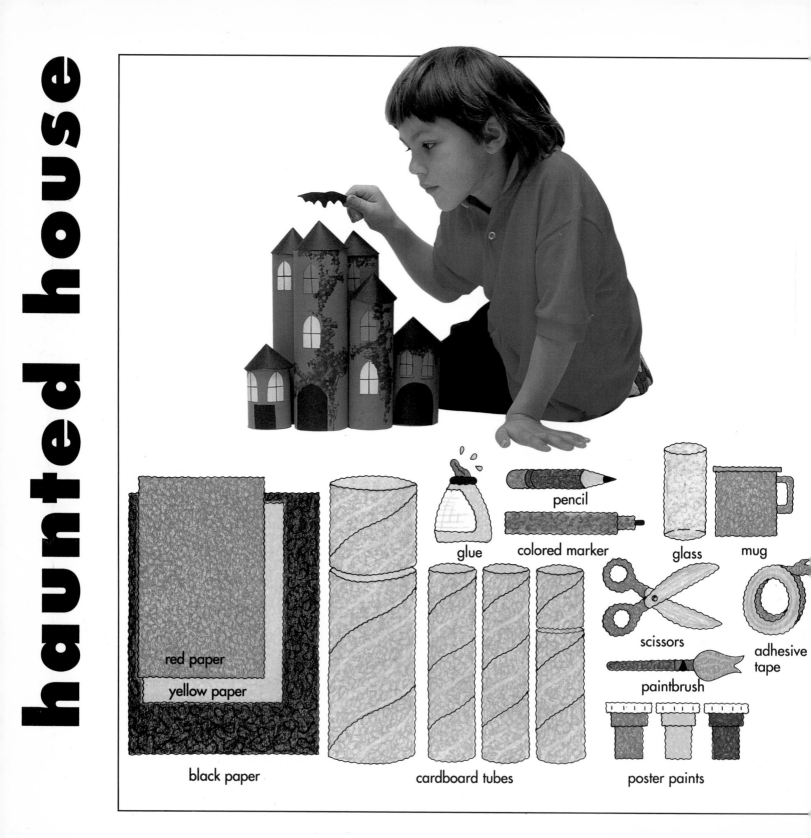

haunted house

red paper

yellow paper

black paper

cardboard tubes

glue

pencil

colored marker

glass

mug

scissors

adhesive tape

paintbrush

poster paints

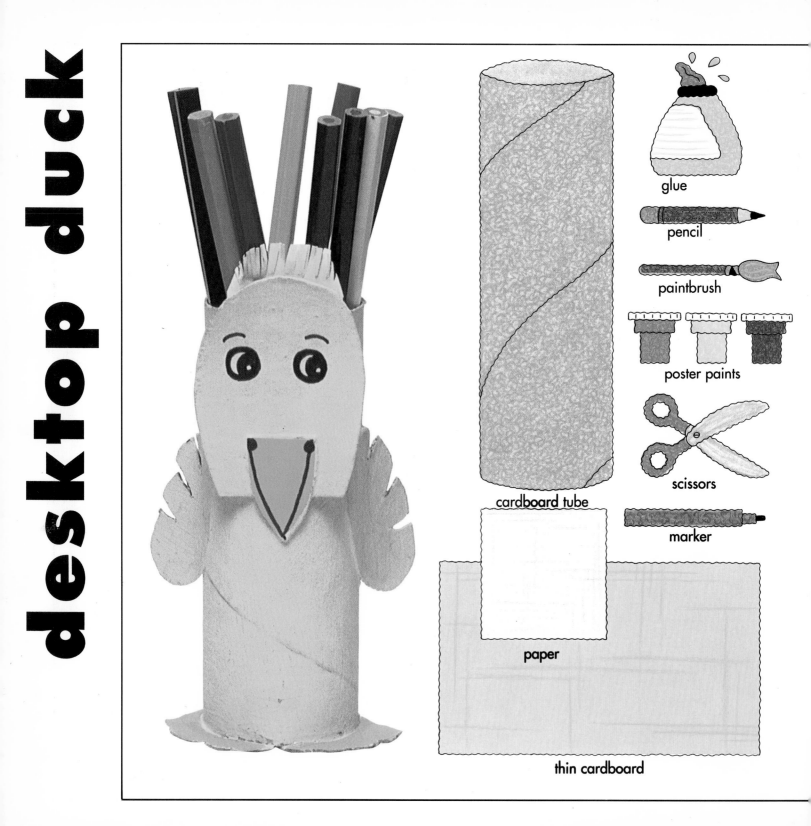

desktop duck

glue

pencil

paintbrush

poster paints

scissors

marker

cardboard tube

paper

thin cardboard

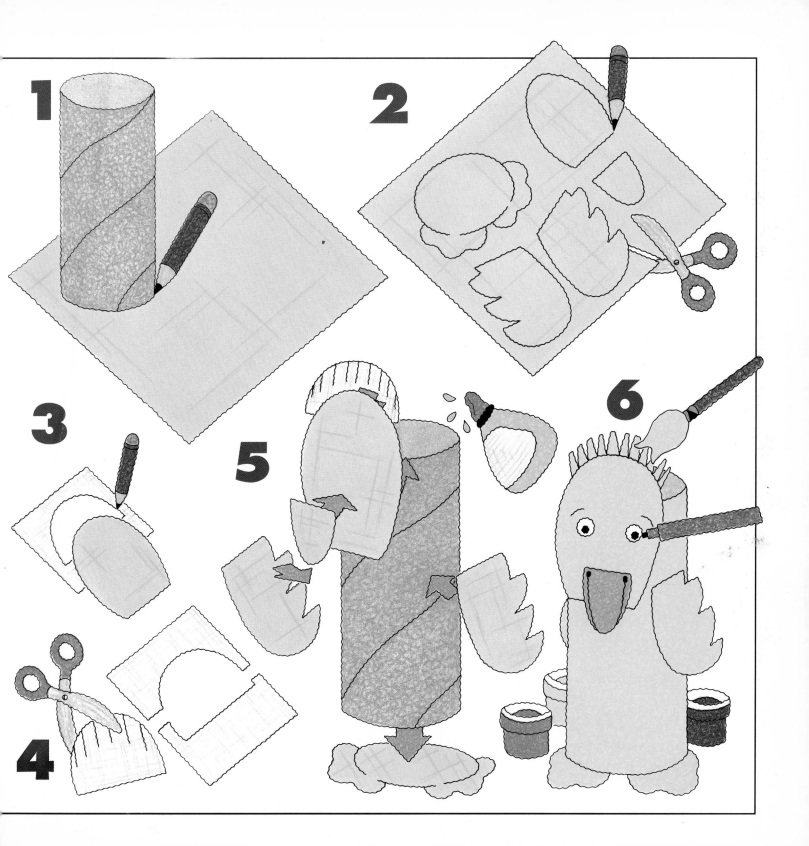

1

2

3

4

5

6

COWS

cardboard tubes

cardboard

glue

marker

pencil

scissors

paintbrush

poster paints

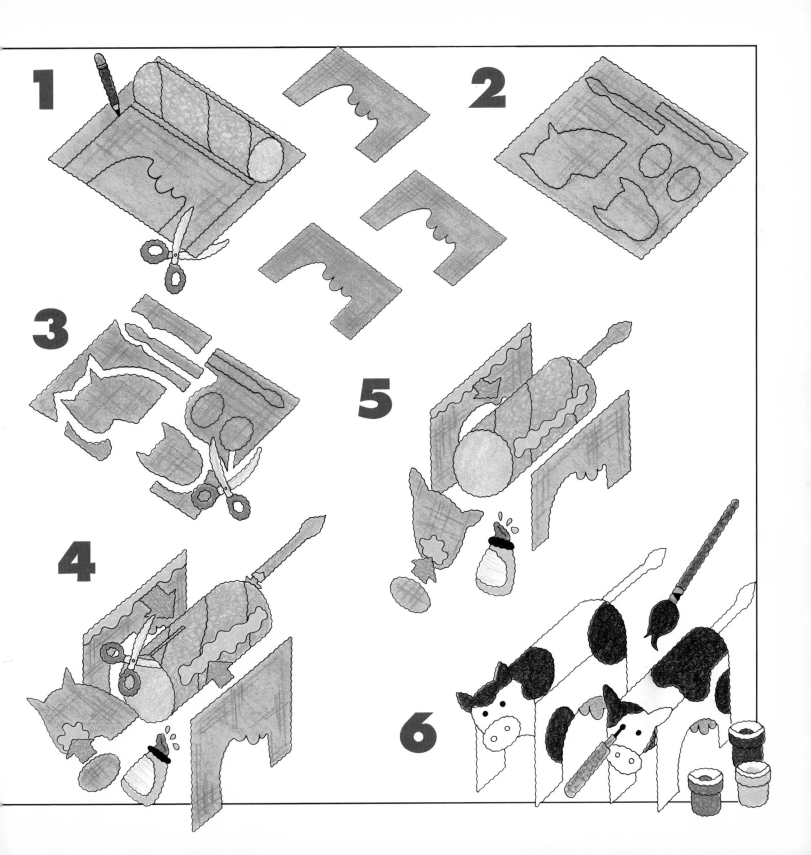

1

2

3

4

5

6

lighthouse

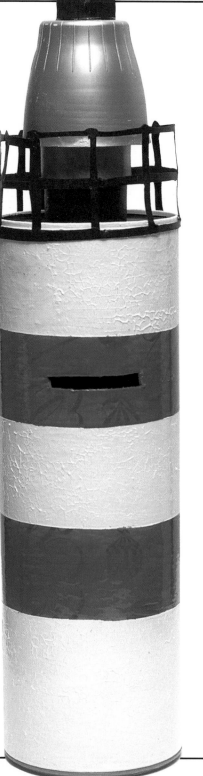

bottle top

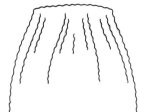

bottle top

cardboard tube

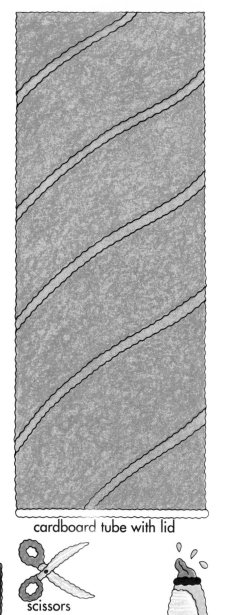

cardboard tube with lid

cardboard or paper

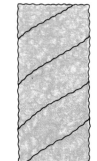

scissors

paintbrush

pencil

glue

poster paints

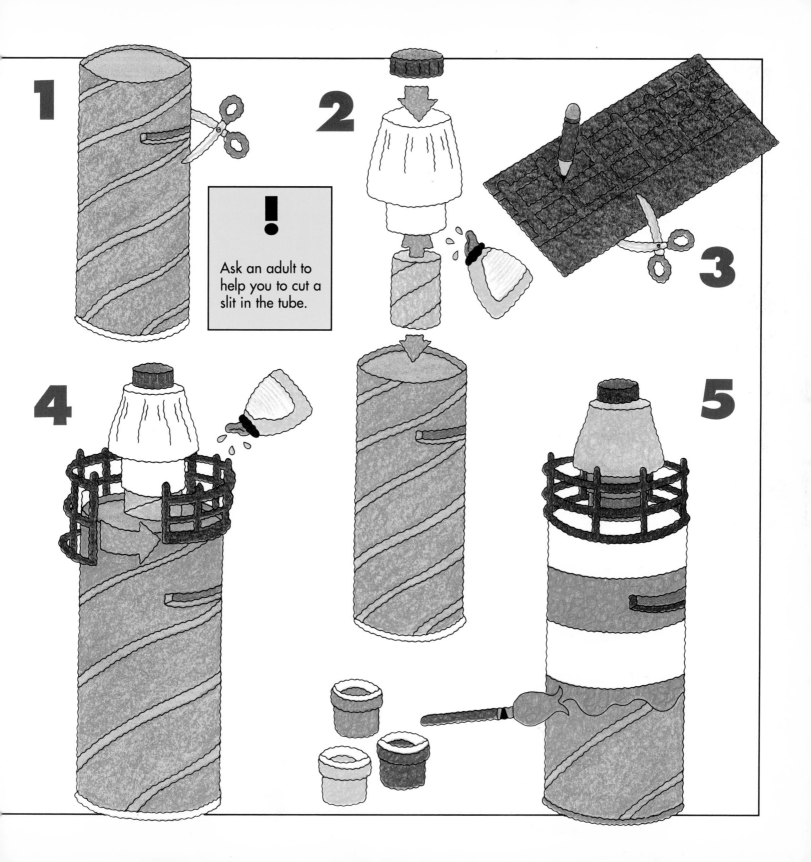

1

!

Ask an adult to help you to cut a slit in the tube.

2

3

4

5

pop-up clown

modeling clay

paintbrush

stick

cardboard tube

plastic cup

felt

yarn

pencil

glue

scissors

poster paints

princess doll

newspaper

paste

cardboard tube

yarn

glue

gold braids

felt or fabric collar

Velcro

adhesive tape

paintbrush

felt or fabric cape

felt or fabric dress

poster paints

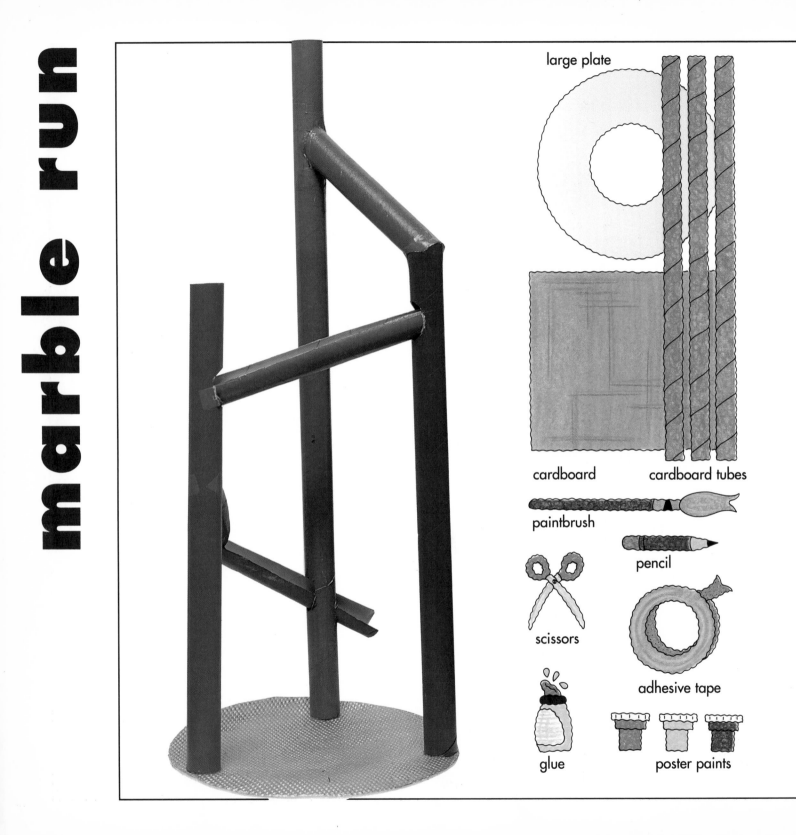

marble run

large plate

cardboard

cardboard tubes

paintbrush

scissors

pencil

adhesive tape

glue

poster paints

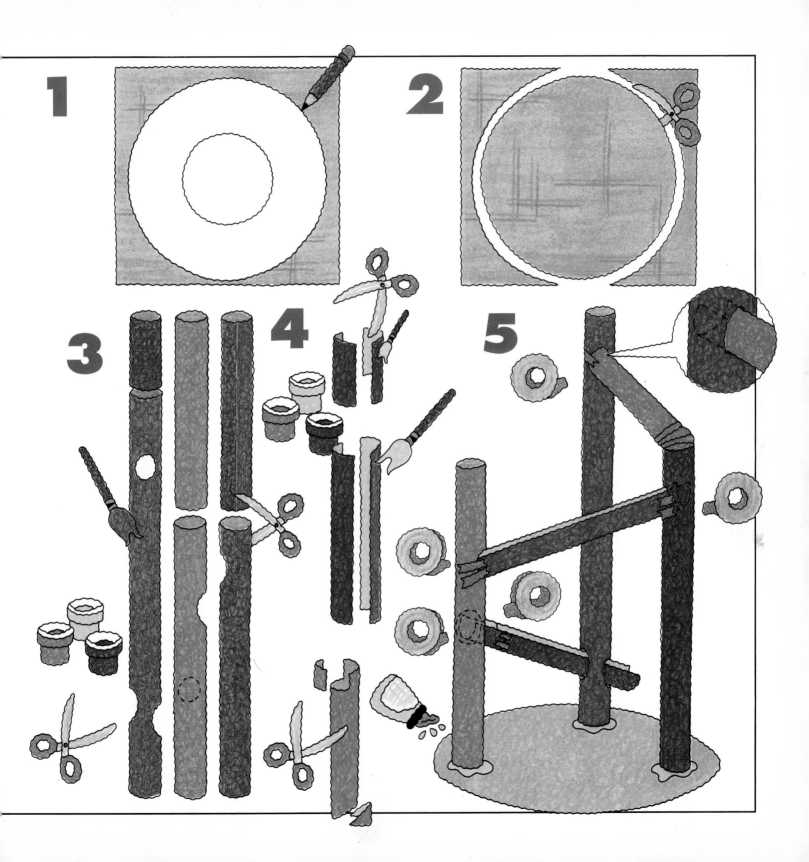

1

2

3

4

5

You can mix the three primary colors to make all the colors of the rainbow. Follow the chart below to mix the colors you want. The numbers on the cups show the proportions of each color you need to make the new color.

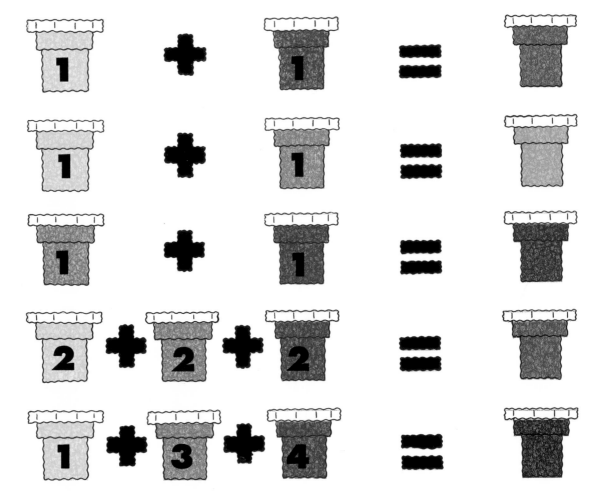

Different types of paint will give different results. Experiment by mixing different proportions of colors. Make sure you wash the brush before dipping it into each paint cup.